heartfelt thoughts about "angel words"...

"angel words" is a sublimely uplifting look into life from the angels' perspective. It touched my mind, heart and soul - made me think, feel, and soar. Thanks to the author/channel, much of what I believe was substantiated and many new lessons learned. This is a timeless work of truth and beauty - what a gift!
    - Rona Jackson, author of "Alphabetize Your Life"

"angel words" is the perfect title for a book whose every word conveys love energy from angels. This love energy comes forth as angels answer ageless questions and wonderments posed by the human mind. Although "angel words" is heart touchingly inspirational in its unconditional love message, it conveys very clearly that we are all "one." And this oneness brings with it an inborn responsibility for each of us to help make this world a better place. Ms. Pizzirani has my deepest admiration for contributing so gracefully in this respect in the writing down of "angel words".
    - Leanna Burns, author of "From A to Z: Feed Your Soul and Lose the Weight," "Soul Beautiful, Naturally," "Living the Soul Dolce Vita," and "Soul Wishes."

angel words

as shared with

jolinda pizzirani

messages for each of us to ponder…

SUMMERLAND
PUBLISHING

First Edition: February, 2006; Second Edition: May, 2007

ISBN: 0-9794585-3-6

Printed in the United States of America.

Table of Contents

angel words: a message

We are all here for a purpose. This is not a new concept to most of us – even if we haven't yet quite figured out what the purpose is. We hope it is something worthwhile – something that will make a positive difference in the world we live in. Maybe just having children that will in turn go out and do something to help others is enough…is it?

If you have read any of my previous novels ("Soul Survivor," "Psychic Princess") or my poetry ("Inspirations"), you know that I am immersed in matters metaphysical. My personal search to learn answers to the questions of why we are all here began in earnest in my early 20's. A dear friend introduced me to books which, rather than answering my questions, only generated more. My thirst to know and learn continued to grow over the years.

I believe that most of my writing does indeed come from my subconscious mind with direct input from "spirit guides," or "angels" if you prefer. I remember many times when the words flowed too easily without my knowing where the story was going or how it would end, to believe they came only from my own creativity.

But writing fictional novels – even if I hoped they would open the minds of others – is no longer enough. I began to have recurring thoughts of publishing a book comprised solely of 'angel words' – messages which might be given to or through me for all of us to ponder. As I sit here about to embark on this endeavor, I hope and pray that the words to come will be meaningful and helpful, and even serve to steer those who are lost in the meaning of their life here on Earth to find their inner purpose.

So let us embark on this adventure together – as physical beings and as angels with messages to pass along to us.

introduction

How shall we construct this piece of literature?

We will talk and you will listen and put forth our words on paper. Simple. That is the way that all of life is – simple – if you take the proper steps to ensure your being in harmony with the Universe, or All that Is. Following your heart and inner mind as you proceed through your lifetime will result in the correct path being taken. We will go into much more detail soon.

Will we know who is providing these answers?

There is no individual essence – or angel or guide, as you call it – that puts forth these messages. We are enmeshed with the Universe in this realm, just as you are in the human form. You are all a part of one another and the Universe, but have been taught to be "individuals" so it is difficult to conceive of yourself as part of a whole. This is one of the many concepts we will try to clarify in this missive.

Can we ask questions?

Certainly, please do. Even those of you reading this for the first time should feel free to concentrate on any questions you may have while reading this, and we will bring the answer to your inner mind without fail. As we are all part of the Universal realm, we continually work together with you to both answer your questions and to pose new ones to your subconscious which will lead you to learning and growing in your lifetime.

Where shall we start?

At the beginning.

the beginning

As part of the Universal realm before birth, each essence is embedded with tendencies and goals which will lead to a general direction for their physical life. Innumerable factors are considered while constructing the basis on which a new life will be embarked upon. In this realm (as in yours, but most of you don't realize it), you have unlimited access to information that will help you make the right decisions as you progress through your lifetime. You literally have a storehouse of data housed in your inner mind before you even begin your adventure in physical life.

In this realm, there are no negative properties, only positive. It is earthly temptations and struggles that lead some humans to seek and embrace negativity.   You are surrounded in the Universe by love and light, knowledge and well-being. You are released into the physical world with the highest of goals set for yourself, and by yourself. Before birth, each essence wishes and plans to reach the utmost of understanding and behavior in the physical state. Some succeed, some even excel further than their highest desired rung of achievement. However, many are bogged down by the daily trials and tribulations of physical life and the people they surround themselves with who unknowingly put forth detrimental influences upon them.

Let us begin with the first years of physical life. You are born into the family and situation you chose while still at Home. Your physical body has the attributes – whether good or bad – that you decided to work with throughout your lifetime. Initially, your family lifestyle and behavior patterns are close to those you anticipated, and may in fact continue much in the same vein as you hoped throughout your lifetime. But much more common, due to the vast number and types of input from those who are closest to you, your lifestyle will begin to change and veer off from your life plan. Each little change brings in turn a myriad of other consequential influences, and you can see how easily your life plan is forever altered.

There is another strong factor in your childhood growth pattern, and that is your ability to make conscious changes which may sometimes drastically alter your current behavior. From birth to perhaps your second birthday, you are much more aware of your own subconscious and in turn its strong connection with Home. Your personal essences – those who you would call "guides" or "angels" – can offer constant help as needed during these first years of physical life. As a baby, you spend much time sleeping and can benefit from this tie with Home much more than in later years. The "channel" is wide open during this time, and only begins to close or narrow slowly as other outside physical elements interfere with your subconscious thought patterns. Your attention span gradually switches from listening to your inner self to paying attention to those around you in the physical realm, especially those who are stimulating you to fit into the mold of human behavior patterns.

Your childhood years let you develop your personality and sense of being an individual. Many factors determine the rate at which you will learn, and again other physical entities will influence how well you do and how you are rewarded for your efforts. But at no time is the link to your inner self severed or altered. You may begin to spend less time listening to your subconscious, as you grow and are taught that only that which you can see or feel is real. Of course, having a spiritual part of your life – no matter which church or type of religion you practice – will be of benefit to your overall well-being. Praying or talking to a Higher Power will manifest the same helpful essences that you were able to connect with as a small baby. It is only how much you listen and believe in what you are being told that will make a difference in how you live your life.

Children's actions are swayed by their peers, teachers, family members, camp counselors, religious leaders, and just about everyone else they hear or see as they travel through life. Just because a child does not have the benefit of wealthy parents and therefore knows only a simple lifestyle does not mean the child has less of a chance to succeed at their goals. We do not need material things in life – or very few in reality -- to be comfortable. Food, clothing, and a roof over our heads will just about suffice. Many extremely successful people have come from very poor backgrounds, and have proven that they are able to achieve their goals by learning from their hardships and stepping up over them as they progress through life to prosperity.

But do not believe that prosperity is the answer to all of your problems. It is certainly not. Unless you have spiritual prosperity, you will leave this life poorer than you can possibly imagine.

It is our hope that these words will assist you in understanding your physical life and help to reconnect you to those at Home who are waiting to help you.

angel subjects

In anticipation of "dictating" this book, the angels periodically gave me subjects to be included. I would jot them down on a slip of paper next to my bed, then add them the next morning to the growing pile of notes. When the time came to begin this book, I consolidated them into the list of subjects you will see here.

The hope is that these are the types of questions you would ask the angels yourself. It is clear, however, that all of your questions may not be included in this edition. Therefore, I encourage you to email your additional angel questions to:

Questions4Angels@aol.com

We will make every effort to publish additional editions of "angel words" that incorporate your queries along with the responses put forth by the angels.

Thank you.

As you walk through your daily life, you tend to settle into patterns of behavior and methods of operation which can operate as if you were on "automatic" with no thought to possible alterations. You get up at a certain time, perform the same morning ablutions, take yourself to school or work, perform your duties according to past experience as to what is expected, float through your evening in keeping with the day of the week, and finally lay down to rest your body for another day. It is almost as if you have become a robot that has been preprogrammed to make it through each day so you may rise in the morning to start again.

If you are reading this book, it is probably because you have begun to question your physical life and where you are headed. Perhaps you have felt in a rut and are striving to understand how you can get out. Whatever the reason, it is all for the good that you are questioning your standard behavior and wishing to learn and grow.

You can start by really thinking about each and every thing you do during the day, from the moment you arise until you lay your head down to sleep at night. Ask yourself why you are doing this, is there a better way to do it, or should you change it – especially if it is a bad behavior – altogether? Really stop and ponder your lifestyle, and honestly evaluate if you sincerely feel you are progressing in the right direction. If you are, then that is wonderful, and you can only improve by following the words in this book. However, if you are not happy with your current way of life, we hope to help you work through the many ways you can make a change for the better.

One way is to pay attention to each and every thing that happens to you. Actions that result from the weather, other people's behavior, or even an inner sense are all very

13

important events to decipher. Very often, these activities will have a special meaning just for you if you are aware enough to catch it. Open your mind to all that is around you and see, hear and feel the Universal connection to each and every thing you do. It may be helpful to even jot down your brief thoughts at the very moment you have them, and then take time later when you can relax and contemplate just what you are being led to understand.

If by meditating on these questions or thoughts you are unable to come up with an answer, simply pose them to yourself just as you are about to fall asleep at night. Your subconscious will bring the answer to you. It may be in the form of a dream, or just a clearer understanding when you awaken. But keep that pad of paper near your bed so you can jot down any hints you receive as you slumber.

Angels are around you constantly, and only have the purest desires to see you succeed with your life plan and goals. Feel free to ask for a sign or direction from them at any time, but be open enough to receive the answer, in whatever form it may come.

Your physical world is full of miracles, and you are one of them.

dreams and nightmares are important

Some of you say you never dream. That is just not true. Your subconscious mind is always active, but much more so while your body is asleep. As you have heard often, your subconscious serves to work out all of the problems you are trying to solve in your daily life, and find solutions to any difficulties you are experiencing. It is because we are often so limited in our conscious state that we cannot find these answers while awake. It takes the subconscious to access the unlimited Universal knowledge "database" and seek to bring the solutions to your conscious self.

So pay attention to your dreams, and also your nightmares. If you do not normally remember your dreams, just tell yourself right before falling asleep that you wish to remember what you dream that night. At first, you may only remember the last dream you had before waking. But eventually, you will be able to recall the important messages being sent through to you all night long. Even if you can't remember your dreams, do not worry since the answers have been planted in your sub-consciousness and will rise to the surface when needed.

Nightmares can be influenced by many physical factors, even including what you ate before retiring. Your physical body may at any time interfere with your subconscious wanderings without notice. But your subconscious is able to deal with such interruptions and carry on. In any event, nightmares are often trying to alert you to a serious situation that you need to address. The severity of the problem may dictate the terms of the nightmare, as your subconscious knows instinctively what will matter to you the most. So pay attention, and ask for answers or help as needed.

essences of family members or friends are inherent in your life and can influence your behavior and feelings

We are not only speaking of essences of those who have passed on, although they are the primary source of influential occurrences. Many times those still in this life who are closest to you can be spiritually with you even when you are apart in physical distance. This will often happen in times of extreme stress, when your loved one will sense your difficult situation and send an immediate prayer for help in your direction. All physical beings are made of pure energy, and the intense desire to help others is one of the strongest forces that exists.

Of course, the essences of those close to you who have returned Home are able to constantly monitor your life's movements and give you a helpful push in the right direction as needed. Sometimes you may be at a crossroads and are having difficulty deciding which way to turn, when suddenly a realization comes to you that makes it clear what the best path is – this is most likely due to assistance from your angels.

Open yourself up to this help, and it will become even more prevalent in your lifestyle. Those who freely believe in and accept guidance from their angels will benefit deeply throughout their lives. Ask for help when you need it – we are here to be of assistance and guide you towards the right decisions.

we are our own judges – IN life and AFTER life

The common conception is that when a physical life is spent, your soul goes to Heaven and is judged by some Higher Power as to its behavior and accomplishments during that physical life span. In actuality, each of you will be your own judge – and jury in some cases – of how you spent your lifetime.

Going back to the issue of all life forms being energy, you can see how we are all part of one Universal life force, whether in physical form or purely an essence at Home. With that image in mind, consider how you are the primary judge of your behavior, even as you are blended with all other essences and All That Is. So though you will answer for any shortcomings, you will constantly be supported and guided by the Universal energy forces around you so you will never feel alone or confused.

Similarly, while in a physical state you will continually be your own judge of how you are doing in life. Subconsciously, you know just what you intended to achieve in this life span, and will judge yourself accordingly. It is through these periodic judgments that you come to realize a need to make changes in your life to hopefully steer yourself back to your original goals. Again, with the intertwined input from all the Universal essences you are a part of, you will steadfastly gain control and redirect yourself appropriately.

forgiveness is divine and life-enhancing

You all know you *should* forgive others, but often it is so very difficult to accomplish. You are trained from an early age to protect yourself against those who might do you harm. You learn to try to avoid situations, where possible, that might result in physical or mental injury. Yet it is inevitable that such damages are done, and as a result you must strive to forgive the perpetrator(s).

The problem lies in the fact that to harbor feelings of non-forgiveness in your heart can sometimes bring a sense of fullness which is mistaken for a thing that is right or just. The longer you refuse to forgive, the stronger the fullness grows and the more reasons you give yourself to never give in. What you don't see is that this fullness is a malignancy that eats away at your inner self, much like a cancer that takes your physical life away.

You live your physical life among all the other people on Earth at that particular time, and must deal with their actions and reactions on a daily basis. How you handle problems when they arise is all part of your basic makeup and what you learn from them helps you grow. By harboring feelings of non-forgiveness against another, you are taking a giant step backwards in your soulful progress in this life. Only through being generous with your forgiveness can you achieve even higher goals that you originally hoped for.

Release the bad feelings from being hurt and fill that space with love and caring instead. Forgiving another is divine, and will certainly enhance your life as you take each step forward on your path. Know that once you have experienced this wonderful feeling of forgiveness, you will have no problem if the need arises again in the future, for you will know firsthand of the inner peace and well-being that results.

Living a physical life is quite complicated, being enmeshed as you are with all others around you and at Home. Just dealing with the needs and desires of those closest to you can seem insurmountable at times. But to demonstrate love and caring for people you don't even know who need help is the most wonderful act of all. By giving of yourself to improve another's way of life, you will gain unbelievable strength to deal with your own problems. It is true that "what goes around, comes around" – you will reap the rewards of your own behavior, be it good or bad.

Performing a physical favor for someone – whether making a monetary donation to a good cause or actually using your own time and talents to benefit others – is certainly a good thing. But even by simply sending thoughts of love and caring to others in their time of need will be just as beneficial to you as to them. Once again, the concept of all living beings as one large force of energy makes it understandable how your sending good thoughts into that stream of consciousness can only result in your receiving goodness in return.

In fact, in the scheme of things, you may even be granted anonymous wishes when you help others. These wishes may be so obscure in your own mind that you didn't even realize they were there until they are granted. This is the wonderful truth about giving and receiving.

share what is close to you

Going back to childhood, most of you are taught to "share" your toys or belongings with others, but you are usually reluctant to truly do so without constant urging from your parents. As long as you get your favorite toy back from the child that your mother made you share it with, you grudgingly agree to try sharing again the next time they come visit.

But if you can truly realize that all material things are just that – "things" – and that they will be of no use to you when you return Home, then it may make it easier for you to release and share them with others. In fact, by sharing things that are most dear to you, you are demonstrating your understanding that there are more important things to do in life than to greedily protect your so-called belongings.

Releasing your hold on your material things will allow you to deal more easily with the emotional and mental progress in your life. This is not to say you should not have any material possessions; only that you should not covet them to the point where they consume your thoughts and affect your relationships with others. If someone else needs something you have and it is not crucial for you to keep it, then give it to them. Again, always remember that "you can't take it with you" …

Prayers are wonderful in that they bypass your conscious mind and connect with your Universal oneness while in your physical state. You tend to let go of your body's restraints and speak to that which is innate within you all. You ask for and receive answers to the questions you have; directions and resolutions are perceived and can be acted upon.

But do not pray solely for your own personal help with whatever problems you are faced with. Pray also for all your fellow beings in your life span, for peace and harmony, for goodness and light. Pray for positive reactions to negative actions of others. By sending your heartfelt wishes into the Universe, you can join all the millions of others who are doing the same and increase the power of your prayers exponentially.

In turn, this increasingly positive flow of energy cannot help but affect all those it touches, especially those who are directly involved in contributing towards it. This is yet another example of how you will reap the rewards of your behavior if it is directed in the right way.

We strongly encourage you to enrich the use of your senses. Each of your senses can be fine tuned to be of the most benefit to yourself and others.

For instance, you hear words and sounds, but with concentration can also hear thoughts and concepts if you practice. You can hear tonal differences in speaking which will increase your understanding of what is being said. As an example, think of a radio frequency. You need to fine tune the dial before you hear what is being broadcast to the fullest clarity. Just a bit to the left or right results in a sound aberration that is almost grating to your ears.

Your eyesight can certainly be improved through the use of glasses, contacts or even surgery. But beyond that, you can learn to use your eyes to see beyond what you usually notice right in front of you. Practice widening your viewpoint to include everything in your line of vision, and then even further. You will begin to see colors and textures that you were unaware of before. Again, an example might be a television set, where you adjust the color and contrast to get the best picture. But your eyes have the capacity to see a million times clearer than the best television set, once you are innately aware of all that is around you.

Touching and feeling an object can be as simple or as complex as you make it. You are used to feeling just the minimum amount of aspects of an item to get an approximation of what it is you are holding. Break free of this ingrained limitation, and truly experience the texture, temperature, shape and consistency of it. You may begin to feel the energy of the item as well, which means that you are becoming aware of your inner life force as it relates to the object you are touching. This is a very good thing.

22

Similar exercises can be used for all other senses, as you learn to fine tune them to the highest degree. Please know, however, that each day may be different and various results can be expected. No two moments or hours or days are alike as far as the energy flow around us, so there will always be a slight change in your sensory perceptions. That is normal. All of us in the Universal life force are constantly changing, growing, learning, improving.

Figuratively speaking, you keep all of your possessions and feelings close to you. It is as if you have a big closet, and in it you have placed all the material things that are important to you, along with all of your deepest feelings, worries, likes, dislikes, desires, dreams, obsessions, preconceptions, knowledge and beliefs. As long as you stand in that closet in the comforting darkness, knowing you are surrounded by everything familiar and dear to you, you believe you are happy.

But only when you are able to fling open the door of your closet and glimpse all that is to be seen outside of it can you begin to expand your understanding of life and your part in it. You may think it requires a lot of courage to step out from your closet of comfort, and perhaps it does take a little, but mostly you need the basic belief in yourself and your part of the Universal life force. Once you have that, the Universe is literally your playground.

Go out and play, have fun, and learn.

rise above your deepest feelings

At some point in your life, and perhaps that is what has led you to read this book, you realize you are actually imbedded in your own revolving circle of beliefs and behaviors. You continue to act and believe the same way you always have, since it is familiar and seems to be safe. It is as if you are walking in the same circle of life, over and over, until you are in a rut and one foot follows the other of its own accord.

When you begin to question your way of life, and wonder if there is more to it than what you have been experiencing, that is the moment of triumph within you that will allow you to truly grow and expand your horizons. You will read the words and thoughts of others, and form your own opinions as to their validity and pertinence to you personally. This is all fine and good.

But you will need to take a step farther and go within your inner self to begin to understand the answers that lie beyond your physical realm. These are the answers that will mean the most to you, since you are only in physical form for a short while in this life span. These are the lessons that need to be learned in order for you to progress and develop and grow spiritually.

What are these lessons? How can you find the answers? There is no set method for any one individual in the physical arena. Each of you is at a different stage in the development of your soul. Just as a child grows into an adult, so does your soul progress through levels of distinction within the Universal oneness that encompasses us all.

Where to start? Meditate from within.

And remember: prejudice will only serve to your detriment.

25

managing the whole theater of life: living, learning, teaching, seeking

Actually, some of your activities during your physical life span are the same as those during your time at Home. You continue to learn, seek answers, teach others, and by doing so, grow within yourself. Like a pyramid, your education encompasses many levels and contributes to your continuous growth and expansion of the whole of the Universe. You progress – and unfortunately sometimes regress – as you make your way through your life. But even to regress can be a way of progressing, as it may take that turn for the worse to enable you to proceed and learn from your mistakes.

The act of living in a physical body presents you with endless opportunities to experience things which will affect your growth and behavior. Breaking a leg, suffering an illness, or any other physical malady brings with it complications and roadblocks for you to overcome. Even if you are not able to overcome the problem, the act of trying to aids in the process of becoming the person you will be tomorrow.

From your earliest moments in the physical ream, you begin learning: what feels good or bad, what brings a positive or negative response from others, how you can get attention or deflect it, and so on. You proceed to be taught by others what is felt is important knowledge to proceed through your lifetime. Facts and figures, methods and procedures, are drummed into your brains in the hope of your being able to cope for yourself when you reach a certain physical age. But it is unfortunately early on during this experience of learning that you forget to rely on the knowledge and innate sensitivity you have within you. Perhaps it is time now for you to recapture that connection.

26

Just as you learn throughout your life span, you in turn are a teacher to others. You may now have a teaching degree and sit in front of a classroom of students, but you begin from an early age to instruct others so that they may perform in a manner that pleases you. Whether it is with your young friends, or later with your own children, you pass along information that you deem important. Again, this is all fine, however it would be so much better if along with this information you encouraged others to seek answers from within, and kept that portal open yourself as well.

You must never stop seeking. Questions, answers, wonders, sensations. This is actually the easiest of them all, since you are born wanting to learn and understand what is happening around you. But you must expand beyond the normal realm of physical knowledge that surrounds you, and seek that which is not always provable by scientific means. Just because you can't see it or feel it, doesn't mean it isn't so.

So, learn to manage the theater of your life. With the myriad of opportunities before you, you will certainly never be bored.

You would think that your life cycle begins with the moment of birth and continues until the moment of death. However, your time in the physical life form is only one of many life cycles you have yet to experience. Each physical life span has its own set of results which contribute to your overall progress in the Universe. As with physical life in general, some results are positive and some are negative, but they all are part of who you are and continue to be. The non-physical periods you spend at Home constitute another type of life cycle, ones that are not necessarily more important than your physical cycles but certainly more fruitful.

Consider one day of your physical life. From the moment you awaken to the moment you drift off to sleep at night you have experienced life in a variety of ways, all of which are part of the building blocks that form your life and behavior patterns. Similarly, your time in non-physical form at Home progresses much the same way, allowing you to learn and grow from the direct environmental and educational impacts around you. At Home, you are quite aware of your part in the Universe, and even more secure as to what you need to learn to progress. Not having a physical body to worry about does make things easier, we do admit.

A very important part of your life span are your sleep cycles. For it is during these sleep cycles that you are back in total alignment with the Universal life force that sustains you. As mentioned elsewhere in this book, whether you remember your dreams or not is not necessarily of dire importance. Your subconscious stores the information shared in your dreams for use when it is needed most. You are usually oblivious of the workings of this inner mind, and until you are ready to learn and understand more, this is probably for the best.

Together, your physical life cycle, sleep cycles, and non-physical cycles join to represent the Universal song of being. If you listen quietly, you can hear it. If you reach deep within you, you can feel it. It is pure love and happiness, and it is there for each and every one of you.

We speak of destiny as that which we are doomed to experience, but that is certainly not the case whatsoever. Instead, your destiny changes with each moment that passes, and each activity your undertake. As with the Universal energy flowing around and through you, your life force is alive and moving and changing at all times. Therefore, it would be impossible to say that one has a set destiny at any particular point in time.

Rather, you make your own destiny – or reality – and it develops, grows, and changes accordingly. You may have begun this physical life with a certain general "destiny" in mind, but you knew then that this was only a desire, not an accomplished feat. So continue to become the best you can be, learn from within and without, and help others as often as you can. This will all help to lead you towards your eventual destiny – whatever that may be.

Of course, your destiny is intertwined with everyone else's in the Universal realm. You are affected every moment by those around you and even those far away from you. Whatever is being put into the Universal life force by one person, will affect the lives and well being of many others. Some in small ways, others in larger ways. So keep this in mind as you think about your next action or reaction – it makes a difference to us all.

Your soul memory is forever complete with the knowledge it has gained over all time. All experiences and lessons are stored as neatly as you would find in an encyclopedia of sorts. However, when in the physical realm, your soul memory is often clouded with the busy goings on around you that your senses are constantly registering and digesting.

So it is like a gift when one suddenly gets a glimpse of an inner soul thought or remembrance. These fleeting moments are so crystal clear and celestial that it may bring a sense of inner peace to the beholder. If you are open to the idea, you will treasure these feelings and recognize them for what they are: a direct link to your Universal essence and its vast store of wisdom.

In actuality, you most likely experience brief spurts of "precognition" or "intuition" on a daily basis, but aren't necessarily aware of it. This is one of the many ways you decide how to function in your physical state – by listening to your inner guidance system. It is only when you distinctly ignore what you are receiving that you may drift from your true course in life.

So pay attention to your thoughts, and you will begin to develop an even finer tuned reception level. This will only enhance and improve on your life experience, and further open your mind to the Universal oneness that surrounds you.

We are all part of God – each and every one of us. Imagine an unending tapestry of souls, rich with colors, textures, differences, strengths and weaknesses. Imagine a nearly invisible golden thread that connects you to the Universal oneness around you. This thread will never break, no matter how much you put strain upon it. This is because you are a part of the Universal whole of existence, as are all physical and nonphysical entities.

Each soul is connected with the Universal tapestry at all times, whether in physical form during a life span or non-physical form at Home. An unbreakable thread leads from your inner self – your heart – to the tapestry of the Universe that surrounds us.

When you are born, your thread entwines with those of your direct family members and those who are constantly around you. As you grow, your thread grows to encompass all of your friends and acquaintances who make a difference in your life. It is as if you are weaving a tapestry of your life. If you could visualize this tapestry, you would see that it is rich with colors that represent the myriad of lives that have touched your own. Each physical entity has a unique tapestry of their own, which continues to become more and more elaborate and beautiful as each day passes.

If you embrace those around you, and find joy in their presence, your tapestry will begin to have a warm glow about it, making it even more pleasing to observe. It will radiate with the unique qualities that are developing within you as a result of each experience you have in your physical life. As new acquaintances come into your realm, they will be welcomed into your tapestry and you into theirs. This is a blending of histories that has withstood the test of time and has proven to be a valuable part of your physical existence.

general "plan" for humanity

Although each physical existence is planned individually before birth, there remains a general plan for humanity at any time in the Earthly realm. Even as each physical entity has mapped it's own challenges and obstacles to overcome in their lifetime, so has there been a global structure laid for the entire population at any one time. This is why the actions of just one human being can and do affect the lives of all others. It is a delicate balance, and one which is always changing and developing.

The overall plan we speak of is monitored and at times directed by the entire Universal force of entities, with the most positive results kept in mind at all times. Even when it seems that the world is in turmoil, it is always a part of the strategy which will yield the most constructive growth on the whole. As individuals in the physical realm, you need not concern yourself with the direction of this general plan except as it pertains to your part in it – which is of the utmost importance. If all physical entities remain cognizant of their effect on the global plan for humanity, it can only lead to a fundamentally improved structure.

tragedy = amnesia regarding differences

By the time you are old enough to read and be interested in this book, you will have seen – unfortunately – one or more terrible tragedies occur in your world. These events make a profound impact on those that it directly affects, but also brings about more widespread repercussions.

One of the most positive is the fact that physical entities will put aside their differences – be it race, religion or general malcontent – and come to the aid of their fellow sufferers. This has been shown time and time again throughout history. In the face of the terrible physical damages suffered by many, there beams a strong pillar of help brought by others wide and far. Tremendous examples of giving and sharing are evident throughout the world. It is in times such as these that the mesh that encompasses us all – physical and nonphysical – is strengthened even more tightly. We are all one; before, during and after this life.

Upon reading this observation, we would encourage you to attempt to maintain this level of compassion and giving to others on a regular basis, and not just bring it forth when a tragedy occurs. By doing this, you will raise your own level of progress within the Universe, as well as positively affect all those who are in your presence throughout this life span.

Take a moment to look at your body. Stand in front of a mirror and study it from your head to your toes. This is the body you chose to occupy before birth, and the way it appears to you now is the result of the way you have maintained it thus far in your lifetime.

Accept that your body is only a temporary vessel for your soul, and you are the captain. Just like the new car or other possession you maintain for length of life, you need to take extremely good care of your body as it is the only one you have during this incarnation.

Discard the belief that you are indestructible, especially when you are seemingly healthy. There are thousands of factors revolving around you at any moment which can and may affect your well being. Just maintaining a healthy eating and exercise schedule is not always enough, although that is certainly a very good practice. In reality, you are at the mercy of everyone in your proximity, every single day.

Let's talk about bad habits. You must see clearly that detrimental behavior (drinking, smoking, drugs, inactivity physically or mentally, etc.) will only serve to shorten the time you have left on earth to accomplish your goals in this lifetime. You are not only hurting your own soul's objectives, but are adversely affecting all of those who are close to you. If you are unconcerned about yourself (which may mean that you have already lost your desire to complete your positive plans for this life), you should think about your loved ones,. Do you want to multiply the negativity of your actions by all those who are affected by it?

Understand this clearly: you can eliminate negative behavior if you desire to do so with conviction. You are stronger than you realize, and that strength together with the powerful support from the Universe can conquer any negative habit your body has acquired.

miracle of life

The miracle of giving life is the basis of God's creation. Souls chose the bodies for their relatively short incarnation on earth, but remain a part of the Universal Oneness for all time – past and present.

God does not deign whether a child will be born in a totally healthy state; this is a decision that is made by the soul itself before birth. If a child is born with a physical defect, or if a body develops a problem during its lifetime, it is because the soul's chosen life plan involved that challenge in it's struggle to learn, grow and progress. Even the pain and suffering this may cause the parents or other relatives and friends is part of the process of growth and understanding for all entities. It is the greatest adversities in physical life that strengthen the soul throughout eternity.

However, it is much more common for souls to enter the world in a healthy, happy body. There will still be plenty of challenges for them to face throughout their lifetime. So, when expecting a child, look to your faith and inner conviction, and let the angels and God stand beside and watch over you.

Even if a physical entity lives to be 100, it is still just a short period of time compared to the eternity we spend at God's side. So place a high value on every moment you live and breathe, and make the most of the precious time you are given to learn and grow.

First, let us discuss what you call "parallel lives." This term has come to mean the concept of living in different time frames simultaneously. Many believe that is why you occasionally have a feeling of "déjà vu" – perhaps you have been there or done that specific thing before, and you are having a quick replay of that occurrence in your mind.

While it is true that when at Home we are able to visit and see all time frames -- from the beginning of time until the present -- it is not exactly true that, for instance, your great-great-grandmother is living in another time frame at the same time you are carrying on with your current life span. For your purposes in the physical realm, time is linear and therefore the past, present and future occupy separate time periods. However, it is possible for a soul -- when deciding upon the path for its next incarnation -- to review past lives (your own and others who are close to you) and evaluate the effects that these physical lifetimes have had on your progress, then proceed with decision making accordingly.

As an example of what we can see from Home, picture three cubes of equal size: one representing the past, one the present, and one the future. Now imagine these three identical cubes rotating within each other. Even though this concept is inconceivable to the physical mind, your inner essence should be able to grasp it fairly easily. This is how all time is observed at Home.

Now as for life on other planets, many of you are correct in believing that it would be virtually impossible for there not to be life forms of some sort in the vast galaxies as they now exist. There are many choices when progressing through your quest for knowledge and truth, and some of them apply to which society you will join when your soul is ready to do so. Much work can also be accomplished while at Home as a non-physical entity, but experiences in various types of habitats are essential in learning through living. Eventually, your advancement will be done mostly on a higher energy level, with little need for a physical body to burden you. So you see you have much to look forward to, and work towards. And remember, your angels and guides are always around you to help as needed – you are never alone.

material and personal success

It seems that it should be quite obvious to you that material possessions are of no import in your life, and yet nearly everyone in the physical realm seeks such pleasures every day until their last. And then, of course, you leave the physical realm to go Home and leave all of your consciously craved assets behind you. Actually, it is not terribly wrong to seek to live your physical life in comfort, as long as it does not become a prerequisite that takes over all of your time, leaving little for the pursuit of true happiness on a personal level.

There have been those in your time who have shunned material things and spent their lives doing good works for others. Mother Theresa was one such special person in your recent time frame. While you admire and even wish to emulate behavior such as that, it is rarely accomplished – again due to the many physical stimuli happening in your life which steer you elsewhere.

But even if each of you could give just a small portion of yourself to helping others, it would make the world a much better place – for yourself and for others. You will find that being generous with your time and, if possible, your wealth to help others will bring you great happiness and peace, much more than you would realize by purchasing another "thing" to take up more space.

Personal success in your physical life means that you are accomplishing the goals you have set for yourself before birth. You did not start out with the intention to get rich, or own many possessions – unless, of course, it was meant to then be given to help others. Some very wealthy individuals, who got that way either by birth into a certain family or by hard work throughout their lifetimes, have strived to repay society and give help whenever possible. These entities are succeeding in their personal quest to progress while in this life.

Please take some time to think about how you are leading your life, and if you are giving of yourself as you know in your heart that you should. It is never too late to change, and as always, we are here to help and guide you.

By the time many of you begin to question what you are really supposed to be accomplishing in your life, you have amassed many layers of behavior patterns that are gradually ingrained on your consciousness. Some of these may be somewhat negative or even dangerous, and need to be recognized and removed.

In order to see your current life and its activities thus far clearer, you need to scrub away the layers; polish the years of scratches from use. It is typical to be weighted down with physical problems and you need to remind yourself of your soul's existence, strength and everlastingness.

To begin, think back to your earliest years in this life span and remember your behavior and thought patterns. Most likely they were simple and direct, and affected substantially by the family members around you. As the years progressed, you learned some good and some bad behaviors, and were influenced by the many people you met as each day went by. Try to recapture your innocent youthfulness, and feel the simple clarity of peeling away all the layers that have covered it all of this time.

Then examine the various layers of behavior that you have accumulated and do your best to identify the good and bad ones. At that point, you should obviously accentuate the positive and if possible, totally discard the negative behaviors. This is all very possible with meditation within your essence, and with a desire to cleanse yourself and become a better person.

Finally, accepting preconceptions without consideration of alternatives will only increase your blockage of the possibilities that abound, and therefore severely narrow your actual scope of reality. So open your minds and expand your beliefs.

Although it may seem to you that you are only interfacing with those whose paths have crossed your own throughout your life span, in fact you are part of the action and reaction of all living beings at any time. Of course, a huge tragedy affects all of us to some degree as we feel sad for the losses of others and many try to come to their aid.

But that is just a small "ripple" of life that touches you compared to the tidal wave of emotion that comes your way when someone close to you is adversely affected. When something like this happens, you are nearly swamped with sorrow and physical and emotional pain as you try to understand and recover from the blow. While you are struggling to keep afloat, you create waves of your own which radiate out and around the world. These "ripples" will touch every human being eventually, in some way or another.

Once you begin to grasp this image, you will see that what follows is that the problems we encounter in life affect us all as part of the Universal tapestry, rather than just those in the immediate vicinity of the tragedy as it occurs. Energy levels fluctuate due to changes in emotions like hope, despair, longing and desire. Similarly, powerful shifts in nature – even when not in your hemisphere – affect all life forms sooner or later.

As an exercise, try to imagine yourself floating out to the atmosphere and looking down upon Earth. Now look around you and view the wonder of the massive Universe surrounding you into infinity. See how small Earth is in comparison with the rest of the Universe? But not matter how small the Earth, or your particular place on it, you are always a part of the whole.

When you begin to accept your connection to all else in the Universe, you will begin to learn to accept your responsibilities and act accordingly.

While at Home, and during the ongoing process of evaluation of your progress through the Universal knowledge base, it may be decided that another incarnation in physical form will be of benefit to you. Please know that this decision is not acted upon lightly, and that great thought and preparation is needed before a life can begin.

Therefore, it is a great gift that you are given when you are brought back to the physical realm, and one that should not be squandered without thought or consideration. Cherish this gift of life and keep remembering how precious it is throughout your life span.

In addition, as you are born into life on the Earth plane, you are given responsibility for taking care of the planet you occupy along with every other being in existence at that time. Any action you may take which results in a negative destruction of any part of the whole of your environment will bring a corresponding negative reaction to you and those around you. You will be reminded of this periodically as various forces of nature begin to suffer from the neglect and even direct misuse of the wonderful world you live in, and the resultant devastation forces you to recognize your part in it.

As mentioned earlier, many behavior patterns are learned from those closest to us when we are very young. Unfortunately, we quickly forget all or most of the valuable knowledge that is part of us at birth and begin to behave badly without remorse at times.

Feeling hatred for a person or thing is unnatural and serves only to bring negative energy full force back to surround you until you release these hurtful sentiments. You are truly only hurting yourself by allowing the natural goodness within you to be overcome with such negative emotions.

For in reality, since you are a part of the Universal tapestry, you are directly related to every other being – physical or nonphysical – and this makes it easy to see how sending out negative thoughts can only serve to hurt yourself.

Your time in the physical realm is relatively short, and for some it may be even fleeting. So do not waste one single moment with harboring negativity; use your valuable time in life form to spread only the positive and you will reap rewards in like form.

seek to learn that which is foreign to you

As a small child, you are eager to learn from every experience. As you grow older, do not lose that interest in learning something new each and every day. Do not be afraid of seeking out that which is foreign or strange to you, as it will most often lead to new awakenings in your inner soul.

Remember, you laid out the path you wished to take in this life before being given the gift of life. There are always many choices to be made as you follow this path, each of which may lead you to a variety of different experiences. Be aware of outside stimuli at all times, and act accordingly. Choosing the path toward lesser material rewards may sometimes result in an even greater benefit to your true self.

Have you ever noticed how different people react to someone with an obvious physical disorder? A few of those in the physical plane are like human angels who offer their help and understanding unconditionally to such individuals. Do not be like those limited people who find themselves uncomfortable when confronting someone with disabilities. These souls have chosen to burden themselves with their physical problems and reap the plentiful benefits and knowledge inherent in living with their condition. On the inside, they are no different than you. Remember, we are all related and part of the Universal oneness.

Finally, do not be one with a "closed" mind; someone who always believes they are right, know better, or know more than everyone else. Such behavior will only serve to discourage you from seeking new knowledge and understanding of the world around you. In fact, there is no one correct answer to almost every question – it is all variable depending on the circumstances. So keep your mind open and continue to grow and learn as your progress through this life span.

you are the editor, director and producer – in addition to the actor – in your life

If you realized just how much capacity you have within you to change the path of your life, you would be amazed and overwhelmed with possibilities. From the moment of birth, you can make whatever decisions you wish that will affect the rest of your life – for good or bad.

Sometimes, you can even stop a certain bad behavior before it is fully ingrained and possibly reverse the negative effects it will surely bring otherwise. You can certainly encourage yourself to perform positive acts which will only serve to add valuable insight to your knowledge base.

You call the shots with your life – no one else does. But that also means that you alone are responsible for your actions and the accompanying reactions. So think about each step you take in life, and be sure you are heading in the right direction for a positive outcome.

angel questions from others

As mentioned in the beginning of this book, many of the subjects discussed were given to me by the angels themselves. However, about a third of the way through receiving their answers, it became clear that I should include questions from others in this volume as well.

Therefore, this section contains many of those questions and their respective answers as given by the angels. As mentioned previously, you may send your question to:

Questions4Angels@aol.com

and it may be included in the next volume of "angel words."

Thank you.

are there orders of angels--cherubim, seraphim, etc?

There are different levels of knowledge gained throughout time which allow some angels to contribute to various ongoing endeavors while at Home. Similar to the levels of schooling attained while you are in physical form, we progress and enlarge our scope of assistance to all others.

The names "cherubim" and "seraphim" have been assigned by those in the physical world who have gained – or retained -- a certain amount of knowledge of life at Home. As it is easier for the human mind to grasp that which is named in order to categorize it, this is of no consequence to us. We at Home do not need labels in order to know our true place in the Universal whole of things at any particular time.

do people really have guardian angels?

Absolutely! Although once again the title of "guardian angel" has been bestowed by those on the physical plane, we are happy to accept it.

A large part of our existence is dedicated to watching over those living their physical incarnations, and helping whenever we can. There is actually a close-knit tie between the angels and those on Earth which corresponds to the tapestry of life mentioned earlier. You are never alone. And if you need it, you may call many angels to your side to assist you, not just one as many presume to be the case.

In times of distress, know that we are surrounding you with our goodness, light and love. Just close your eyes, and you may see the bright white light of Home, radiating warmth and helpful, healing waves from all of us as it envelops you in a protective cocoon. Welcome this assistance, join with all that is around you, and accept the benefit of our help as you need it.

the presence of angel-type beings in every major religious system of beliefs seems to argue that humans have a prior knowledge about the existence of angels. -- is this true or do we somehow learn it as a cultural thing?

The answer would be "both." At birth, your inner self has much of the knowledge garnered through your previous experiences on the earth plane and at Home. However, as mentioned earlier, much of that information usually slowly disappears from memory as a child's mind begins to be more and more occupied with everyday physical events.

So you certainly are born with knowledge of angels – a term which applies to all of us once we return Home, and also to some in the physical realm. You see, it is possible for angels to briefly visit Earth in a form which appears as solid as any other life form. This happens only on special occasions when their direct presence is needed to accomplish an important goal or pass along a vital message. This is another way you in the physical realm may learn (or "relearn") about the existence of angels – by having a direct experience with one such as this.

And finally, individuals who are close to you as you age will certainly add to your beliefs about all such things as Heaven, God, Angels and religion in general. When young, you are like an empty vessel, just waiting to be filled with knowledge. It is hopeful that you will accept only the most positive and productive of this information as truth.

how can we get better acquainted with our own personal angels?

Luckily for you, you do not have just one "personal" angel in your corner. You are surrounded by the essences of many angels at any one time. And the specific nature of these angels may change from time to time. That is to say, at one point in your life you may need the assistance of angels to help with your health while at another time you may have concerns which are best served by other angel essences.

The most important point here is that you remember that each of us is part of the whole of the tapestry of the Universe. Therefore, you already are "acquainted" with the angels, as you are woven into the very fabric of life itself.

Know yourself – truly – and you will know the angels around you.

is it possible that those who loved us on earth take on this angel/protector role once they have reached eternity and continue to bless us with their love and watchful care?

Certainly, when you leave the physical plane and return Home, you will retain the closeness and ties with those you loved in your last life. You will naturally want to stay close to them and protect them. With time, you will gently be led to understand that it is not necessary for you to constantly watch over those specific loved ones, and that you can better serve them and all others by proceeding with your quest for knowledge and goodness overall.

This is not to say that you will ever forget those who you were close to – that is just not possible. At Home you will be rejoined with the essences of all those who have passed before you, including those that you were near to in previous incarnations. Your vision will be enlarged to see that you can never have too many loved ones, or feel stronger about one than the other. You will learn to love unconditionally, and without having to choose one essence over another.

In this way, the whole of the tapestry of angels can provide the love and watchful care you speak of to all that are in need of it at any time.

why are there huge catastrophic horrors like the tsunami and Hurricane Katrina? why do tiny, innocent babies have to die?

Forces of nature on Earth are intertwined with many things, including treatment of the environment which many of you are beginning to understand. Of course, there are some parts of nature which are developed on an ongoing basis as a result of thousands of years of activity. But more and more natural disasters are the result of human activities which are harming the world you are given to live in.

Although angels cannot prevent these types of terrible tragedies from occurring, we can help in many other ways. The souls of those who lose their lives are gently helped on their way Home to begin the next phase of their development. Those who remain on Earth who were related to those who perished are given special attention to help them begin to recover and go on with their important lives. And perhaps most importantly, it is the hope that lessons will be learned from these tragedies which will add to the growth and knowledge base of those left on Earth which will, indeed, make the world a better place.

As far as the death of tiny, innocent babies, we can only say that these events have multiple reasons for happening. First, the soul of the baby had made the decision before being born to live a short life. Even such a minimal time on the Earth plane has a definite effect on the growth of the inner self. And second, and perhaps more evident, is the effect of the baby's death upon those close to it. This is one of the most trying experiences for anyone to go through, and only by finally accepting the path of all life and our parts in it can we gain the insight and truth of why we are put on the physical plane in the first place: to learn and grow and improve our inner selves.

Believe in yourself, in those around you, and in the Universal tapestry of life. And if you have suffered such a terrible loss as a child passing on before you, be assured that it is only the physical body which is gone. The true essence of that entity exists forever and is a part of you always.

does God truly forgive the most horrific sins of a non-believer if he asks for forgiveness on his death bed?

Those who commit terrible sins, whether they are "non-believers" or not, must learn from their mistakes before they are able to progress. The worse the transgression they committed, the longer it usually takes for the soul to regain a sense of what is right and understand why they did what they did in their physical life.

But know that even the most heinous of criminals is given time to find this knowledge. No one is denied that gift, since it is impossible to remove or let go of a part of the Universal whole. When enough progress has been made by this essence, they may desire to be returned for another incarnation to go through new experiences which will aid them in their course.

In addition, there is the fact that the victim(s) of such crimes must be magnanimous enough to take on such a role in their physical life. Their souls will not only gain valuable personal experience through suffering such an event, but will assist in the education of all others by example. This is an extremely complicated concept with many consequences to consider, so it is not undertaken lightly by a soul before birth.

As difficult as it may be to understand, there is a reason for every occurrence in the physical realm. So trust your inner self to know how to react to such atrocities, and seek goodness and truth each and every day.

how can God hear our prayers when we merely 'think' the words in our mind and do not even speak our prayers aloud?

When at Home, you are in a non-physical form which we call an essence. Although your essence, or soul, retains all knowledge it has learned throughout time, you have no need of a physical body to limit you. All contact is made through non-verbal communication and understanding is complete and immediate. Again, as a part of the Universal whole, you are innately able to "see" the truth and act upon it accordingly.

Similarly, it is not necessary for those in the physical realm to speak aloud when praying or contacting those at Home. Of course, you need to concentrate on your thoughts and remove any outside noise or clutter from your mind in order to be most effective. Just like a radio signal, once you have a clear channel for transmission, you will be heard just fine.

are angels the same age as when they die or are they the best year of their life?

Without a physical body to encumber you at Home, you have no concept of "age" or concern about "how you look" as you do in the physical realm. However, your soul will have the benefit of all of the knowledge you have learned thus far in your progress. Even if you suffered from Alzheimer's late in your physical life, your memory will be totally restored once you reach Home.

You will be able to process all of the input you received from your most recent incarnation, and garner the fruits of your experiences now that you have returned Home. At first, you may fondly remember certain parts of your life as the most pleasant and life-affirming, just as you may sadly recall events that brought your despair and unhappiness. Every experience serves to enrich the fiber of your being, once you are able to assimilate and understand it.

You will also have the information you gained throughout all time to benefit your evolution. How you use that data is up to you, but as a part of the whole you will be gently guided as to the best avenues to achieve your goals.

Heaven, or Home, is indescribably wonderful and yet complex. There are so many layers of activity going on at any one time that it is impossible to put it into words which could be understood by those in the physical realm. So much of what you feel and experience while at Home is based on the non-physical that you can now only begin to imagine the infinite possibilities that await you.

The Universal tapestry of life is forever rippling with activity, growth and goodness. The colors are ever-changing and beautiful, like a million rainbows combined. The sensations are innumerable, all without the benefit of a physical body. You will soar to new heights with each incarnation and continue to learn and grow.

Without the worries and concerns of a physical life, you are free to explore and begin to understand the many levels of knowledge that are available to you. It is truly a wondrous place,

No. Those in the physical realm that commit sinful actions will begin to suffer for those actions while still in the physical state. This happens because the innermost essence is aware of these negative events, and begins to fight the physical longing to commit them. This causes a turmoil within the physical being which normally results in deterioration of their health and/or emotional state. The culmination of this type of behavior is a painful struggle within, sometimes leading to terrible reactions for the individual.

Certainly, when this type of soul finally passes over to the non-physical realm at Home, they are given immediate assistance to deal with their transgressions. But the idea that there is a separate "place" where these troubled souls go after an incarnation is incorrect.

how do you feel about those who don't believe in you?

Most of those in the physical realm have some type of beliefs – good or bad – when it comes to angels. However, even those who are total non-believers are not thought poorly of at Home. These individuals have simply either forgotten all of their inner knowledge upon birth, or have chosen to lead a life of religious deprivation for a reason that they believe will contribute to their growth.

In addition, we realize how difficult it can be for certain individuals who are overcome by society's set rules for behavior. For instance, if you commit a crime and are put in a cell, you are deprived of your freedom. Terrorists may be trying to rob you of this same freedom using other methods. These types of events manipulate the physical body's ability to sustain wishful behavior, therefore resulting in a diminished capacity for positive understanding and belief in a higher power. This is well understood and taken into consideration here at Home.

More importantly, we do not recognize negativity as such at Home, so therefore we do not suffer from worries such as these. When you return Home, you are wonderfully freed from such mundane concerns. Instead you are encouraged to spend your time learning from the array of positive energy levels that abound here.

Certainly, another incarnation on Earth or elsewhere might be chosen if it would be of benefit to one's learning curve. As mentioned earlier, such choices are made with great care and collaboration with others here at Home. It is not only your future that would be affected, but the futures of those who will be in the physical plane at the same time as you and indeed, every essence in the Universal family.

As far as wanting to return, you are probably asking due to your strong ties to the physical realm you now dwell in, and the close family and friends you have made which you are reluctant to leave behind. A physical existence offers a tremendous amount of experiences that can be learned and added to your knowledge base. In fact, in some ways, you cannot truly gain certain types of knowledge without a physical incarnation taking place.

But while at Home, you will have unlimited opportunities to improve yourself, while using your experiences in the physical realm as a basis for your future endeavors. Again, as we are all part of the whole, you will never miss another person's presence just because you are at Home and they are still in the physical realm. As they are part of you and you are part of them, it is impossible. So make the most of your physical life and bring as much joy and happiness into the world as you possibly can in the limited time you are there.

how did you achieve angel status? Is "angeldom" in my future?

While it is true that there are different levels of knowledge at Home in the non-physical state, each and every essence is considered an "angel" when you pass into this realm. How you use your awareness while here is up to you. Some essences progress faster than others, although that is not necessarily a good or bad thing. There is no measure as to how you accumulate your knowledge, nor how you use it, except that only positive change is desirable.

Some essences at Home retain a stronger focus on the physical plane than others, and therefore tend to stray closer to certain people, places and things to aid in their development. This is fine, and can be of benefit to the essence itself as well, but is not mandatory whatsoever. So you will have to see what your desire is when you arrive Home. It may be you will release your physical ties quickly and happily, and proceed with excitement into the wonderful sea of learning that is available to you here. Or you may wish to go ahead at a slower pace and keep a closer watch on what is happening in your former abode.

Either way, you are the one that makes these choices, as always, as you are the one who will benefit.

how can we contact our loved ones over on the other side?

We assume by "the other side" you mean in Heaven, or here at Home. As we have explained earlier, those who pass over remain a part of the whole of the Universal family. It is only their physical body that is released, so they may be free to take advantage of the energy levels of learning and proceed with their progress.

As long as you are quietly meditating on your message to someone who is at Home, they will receive your thoughts immediately. If you are open to it, your loved one may even visit you, especially in your times of extreme need. This visit may not be in the form of an appearance that you can see (although sometimes it is), but more often as a field of energy that you can feel surrounding you for a few moments.

Also, an essence here at Home may leave a particular object that will be a sign to you that they are near, bringing you peace and comfort. Just know that we are all part of one Universal family and we are with you every moment.

If you are looking for physical proof that angels are around you, you may not find it. There are instances, as stated in the previous section, where a familiar object may be left where you can find it or a certain song will play on the radio when you are feeling down. These occurrences certainly may have been 'encouraged' by one or more angels watching over you.

But you should try to feel at ease without such physical signs, knowing that you are part of the tapestry that touches us all. Know that it is impossible for you to be alone.

If you like, you may try to meditate quietly and speak to those at Home that you care about. It is very likely that you will feel the energy enveloping you, sending love and caring your way.

Rarely, those in the physical realm are given a glimpse into the Universal spectrum and may see or feel the extraordinary warmth and love emanating from the pure white light that is all Goodness and envelops us all. This usually happens when one is in a limbo state – sometimes due to illness or trauma – between the physical and non-physical realms. But this wondrous sensation can also be obtained through pure meditation and connection with those at Home that are all around you. This is indeed a gift to be treasured, but not to be sought out for personal reasons.

are there different angels to help us with different areas of our lives?

No, all essences at Home are available to assist and guide you at any time. Of course, there may be a particular essence that has a specific reason for helping you with a certain problem you are encountering, and that action would add to the progress of the essence as well as your own.

In addition, the angels that help you may have different experiences which might dictate exactly what type of aid they send your way. It is never a clear cut action or reaction, which is why our Universe is so complex and compelling.

It is hoped that each person on Earth will try to live their life to the best of their ability, thereby enabling them to progress up their knowledge ladder to the next step. Then, when you are at Home after finishing your current incarnation, you will be immersed in a multitude of educational and motivational areas that will assist you in your progress, and in turn those of others still in physical form.

We are all part of the whole, even as we each have our own very special and individual qualities and abilities. Use yours to achieve your goals and help to make the world a better place.

how do angels communicate with us?

Although we are communicating our thoughts through this book at this particular moment, there are many different ways that we can get our messages across to you on the physical plane. And if you are wondering, every physical entity can hear angel words, but as a prerequisite they must be open to receiving our messages and of a nature to handle them properly.

Normally, we communicate in response to prayers, questions or concerns raised by those in the physical realm. Our answers may be discerned literally (as in the case of this book), as well as through the dream state, meditation, or other methods.

As in the Universe, there are too many variables to list here. Just know that we are listening and responding, each and every moment that passes.

why are you in contact with us?

As we are all part of the Universal whole, contact is constant.

However, we believe you are asking for a less literal answer. If you have not asked for our help, it is unlikely that you will sense our presence, although we remain close to you nonetheless. There are times when we will send thoughts to you which you will believe come from your own subconscious. This happens in particular when you have lost your way in life and need definitive direction.

As for our words in this book, this is one of many avenues we are using to spread the knowledge which will benefit you as you proceed through your physical life span.   If you are reading this now and find our words to be of merit, it will mean we have accomplished a portion of our efforts thus far.

If you now set aside this book and send us a gentle thought, we will respond in kind to confirm our presence. We wish you peace, joy and happiness always.

did you ever live in the physical realm?

Every essence at Home at one time lived in some physical realm as it is part of the base to our knowledge pool. Without experiencing life with a physical body and all the incumbent joys and sorrows, we would not be able to attain the level of wisdom needed to progress.

Many essences require several, and in some cases quite a few, incarnations before they are able to acquire the needed knowledge base for them to move on. As you have probably seen during your own lifetime, some people learn faster than others. Some seem to ignore a lesson that is repeatedly shown to them over and over again. Even with the best laid plans for an upcoming incarnation, there are far too many possible directions that you can chose to go in while in the physical state for there to be a sure success to your particular lifetime.

So, it is try, try again, until you get it right. But that is also part of the Universal plan: those with repeated incarnations will be able to provide certain guidance to others in the areas that they have been successful in learning. For example, let's say that is a person who has a problem with money (of which there are many), but otherwise is a giving, caring individual. Although this person may need to return for a few more incarnations to conquer their monetary problem, they will be able to guide others who need help learning to be giving and caring.

It is a complex Universe, but each and every one of us is an important and necessary part of it.

why do we say "all men are created equal" when in reality we aren't?

You are right, in that each physical life is begun with different abilities and disabilities, diverse physical makeup, and various family configurations – all of which affect their life in some way. But once again, remember that these choices were made quite some time before the life was begun, and are all a critical part of the life plan developed in detail by the essence itself.

However, if you are solely referring to the material status one attains during a physical lifetime, that has little import in the Universal scheme of things. Greater material wealth can be a help or a hindrance to one's development. Only those who use their wealth to help others and make a positive difference in the world around them will ultimately achieve greater knowledge and understanding through their generosity and kindness.

Similarly, the burden of being famous in a particular lifetime brings to the forefront the need to make correct decisions as you proceed through life, as each and every movement will be scrutinized by the many who observe you. Even being considered beautiful over many others has the potential to create goodness or sadness, depending on how this beauty is shared and used for the best purposes. Surely, we all know that vanity is a part of nature, but it must be tempered and even appreciated by the person it is bestowed upon in order not to take away from their inner soul beauty.

why are some angels quite simple in their manifestations while a few others are more expansive in their range of light?

Few of you in the physical realm will even see an angel once during your lifetime. This is not an everyday occurrence, and requires a complicated set of circumstances to be in place before even a tiny manifestation can take place.

The fields of energy inherent in the physical world can occasionally be used by an angel wishing to present itself in the physical realm for a moment. The brightness or expansiveness of this manifestation depends on the many prerequisites needed at that moment.

What you don't realize is that there are constantly angels all around you, if you could only but see them with your human eyes. So do not dwell on the wish to physically see an angel before you; we are here always and forever and surround you with love and kindness.

why do angels vanish the very instant that they are seen and recognized?

As explained in the last question, a complex set of prerequisites are required for an angel to be seen by a human's eyes even for a moment. It is due to the fluctuation in the energy fields that makes it appear that an angel has vanished. Remember, we are around you always, even if you can't see us.

So the ability to see an angel on Earth is not governed by whether or not they are seen or recognized, although it may seem that way to those on the physical plane. Realize that you personally affect what is happening in the energy that surrounds you at any moment, and that may also contribute to whether or not an angel is able to show itself in your realm.

So relax, and seek to believe in your heart and inner soul that we are here for you, and that it is not necessary to physically see things to make them 'real.'

how is it I have perfect vision when I see angels since at all other times I must wear either glasses or contact lenses to correct my vision to 20/20?

Because when you are open to seeing angels, and the energies are aligned in their complexity to allow such an event, you are seeing with your soul and not your physical eyes. You will notice that when you meditate, your inner vision is not impaired whatsoever by the physical limitations of your body's eyesight.

Remember that your true essence is your soul and that you will continue on your progress even after your current physical body has expired. You do not need your body to see and feel what is truly real in the Universal realm; it is known to you at your deepest core of knowledge.

Do we have to relinquish our preconceived ideas on this earthly plane to allow angels to enter our lives?

Those in the physical realm who are enmeshed in their earthly endeavors may not be cognizant of their true reality in the Universal realm. Many people go through their lives without ever finding this truth until they are back at Home where they begin to sort through their life experiences and develop their future path accordingly.

However, there have always been those who seek knowledge outside of their set physical surroundings. People like this grow to be more and more open to learning about the soul and that which is not physical in nature. Perhaps these people are the same ones who have lived many incarnations and are now finally ready to embrace this type of knowledge while on the physical plane.

But in any event, no matter what your level of inquisitiveness or the state of belief you currently maintain, you are Blessed and no particular circumstances must exist for angels to be around you always. We are here for you, now and forever.

do angels help teach peace to everyone in this disturbed world? Or just the ones that are open to the work?

Living peacefully with one another is certainly a major project that has been ongoing for all human time. However, even those who commit the worst crimes against society can be open to divine guidance, and it will be given without condition when sought after.

Then there are the many who are benevolent and worshipful who certainly help us in our efforts to maintain a peaceful existence for you on the physical plane. Sadly, it has not yet happened that there is enough goodness to overcome the evil that exists and we must continue our struggle in this regard.

Finally, there are those who profess to be prayerful, but in truth neglect to truly commit to their ability to do good for others. We are constantly with each of you and supporting you as best we can so you can hopefully follow through on your promises.

You may not think you or someone you know is "open" to hearing us, but we communicate on many levels – spiritually and emotionally – and are successful in assisting you even if you are unaware of our help.

how do we on Earth teach the goodness of life to those who are not aware?

The problems the human race has developed over years and years of existence stem from learned behavior patterns which are passed down from generation to generation. Occasionally, a youth is strong enough to veer off from that taught by their parents, but it is not always easy to do so.

In order to be a teacher of goodness, one much be an exemplary student first. So use your good actions to demonstrate the kindness you would expect from others, and this will continue in a ripple effect to help us all.

And remember, there is no separation from those on Earth to those of us at Home. We are all part of one infinite Universal tapestry, and thus our actions and reactions can make a real difference to us all.

… like when bad things happen to good people -- like when our 3 year old son died of cancer before his life even started, and bums on the street seem to go on forever?

This is a heartbreaking comparison of seemingly unfair circumstances, but deserves to be discussed. The reality is that these are two separate entities with different goals and plans set for them. Your child passed at such a young age to learn precious lessons only a drastic occurrence such as this can impart. As difficult as it is to understand, this was your son's chosen path which he set in motion before he was born. He did, however, also choose you for his parent and that is an extremely important part of his heritage as well.

How this child affected your life before and after his passing all contribute to the physical reality that existed then and as it does now. Sadly, it is often the most cruel of circumstances that results in the strongest reactions from those on Earth. How you chose to deal with his passing is a big part of how you are living the rest of your life. If you were able to celebrate his brief time in the physical realm even for a few moments, and cherish what he gave to you, then you will be better able to cope with your future as it unfolds.

Conversely, a bum on the street doesn't usually affect many others as he is typically alone and has little interaction, physical or emotional. His sad life will be remembered by few, if any, and he will pass on to find that he squandered the gift that was given to him. But he will learn from those mistakes and go on from there. Try to realize that prolonging the life of

81

someone so destitute is not necessarily a welcome thing for them. All living things deserve a chance to do their best; not everyone is able to accomplish that.

First, you must recognize that only your physical body is no longer viable – your true essence, or soul, will never die.

As you progress through your life on the physical plane, a portion of each and every day is spent reflecting on your past and future, although you are most likely not aware of it. It is as if you are reviewing a checklist of your goals and ambitions in this life, evaluating where you stand, and what adjustments need to be made. Most often this takes place in your sleep state, when your waking mind is at rest and can allow your inner self to take over.

Therefore, you are always prepared to relinquish your physical body when the time comes to return Home. We should mention here that if the end of your physical life includes a terribly painful passing, your essence will depart just prior so that your body's pain does not register with your soul. At that point, your body has served its purpose for that incarnation on the physical plane, and hopefully you will let it rest in peace. However, there are some souls that have more difficulty than others in releasing themselves from what was their temporary home on Earth. Their struggle is aided by others, both at Home and on the physical plane, until they are encouraged to let go and return Home to do their true work. Please know that this does not happen often, as most souls are quite happy to be back Home and finished with their physical life at that point.

You may have read accounts by others who have gone through what is called a "near-death experience" in your realm. Seeing a white light and sensing the presence of loved ones are a common thread in these accounts. These individuals have indeed seen a glimpse of what lies ahead when they leave the physical realm. The white light represents the indescribable goodness inherent at Home, and along with it you feel a love stronger than any which you ever felt while on Earth. You will be overjoyed to be returning Home where you are able to fully recognize all of your past experiences – both in the physical and non-physical realms – and put your newfound knowledge to its best use. You will work at your own pace, as everyone is different – which by the way is one of the many blessings of our Universal tapestry of oneness. We are one, yet unique individuals at the same time.

Each essence will then begin to fully incorporate their recent incarnation's experiences and newfound knowledge into their part of the Universal tapestry, making it even stronger with each passing moment. As you progress, you are given new goals to reach, keeping you very busy and fully involved with the many projects going on at any one time. Your strengths will be used to their best purpose, and your weaknesses will be worked on with the help of others around you.

The life of a soul is never-ending, and your blessed place in the Universal tapestry of life is permanent and of the utmost importance to us all, no matter how big or small of an impact you make upon it.

So live your life to the fullest, love and help others, and do your best to help make the world a better place. We are here to help you.

a message from Jolinda

This has certainly been a wonderful and stimulating experience for me, and I hope these angel words will have some positive meaning to you as well.

I wanted to share the following with you: I have said the Lord's prayer every night since I was about 5 years old when my mother taught it to me. I always begin with "Our Father, Who Art in Heaven,..." About midway through transcribing this book, for no conscious reason whatsoever, I began my nightly prayer with "Our Family, Who Art in Heaven..."! I remember stopping myself and smiling, thinking that this is a truism that more of us should embrace, then corrected myself and went back to "Our Father..." in deference to tradition. But I admit this momentary amendment made me smile to myself.

I encourage each of you to send your questions for the angels to:

Questions4Angels@aol.com

for inclusion in the next edition of "angel words." I know there are untold uncertainties that need reflection upon, and welcome your input.

Bless you all, as part of my Universal family.

85

Jolinda has published several other works, including her "Soul Survivor" and "Psychic Princess" novels and her poetry compilation entitled "Inspirations."

Jolinda lives with her husband in California. Her main goal – *in this life* – is to heighten others' awareness via the written word as to choices and circumstances we all face as we travel the path towards our individual destiny. You are invited to join her in this quest by reading her novels and poetry.

Visit Us Online at *www.summerlandpublishing.com*

ALSO AVAILABLE FROM
SUMMERLAND PUBLISHING

Bringing you books to help "make the world a better place."

"Soul Survivor" by Jolinda Pizzirani is a metaphysically-oriented story of a doctor who learns he is dying and decides to participate in an experiment to "prove" life after death. His intention is that if life after death is proven to exist, the way in which people live their physical lives might change dramatically. In this day and age of uncertainty and strife throughout the world, we all need to look to our inner selves as well as our individual religions for spiritual guidance and help. Readers of "Soul Survivor" will be enlightened as to the possibilities that exist, and how these particular characters are guided by their inner selves.

U.S. $15.95 / CAN. $20.95   ISBN 0-9794585-0-1

Jolinda Pizzirani, author of "Soul Survivor" and the "Psychic Princess" series, takes us into her meditative realm and offers inspirational messages to all who seek Universal knowledge in this life. *"Inspirations"* is a collection of metaphysical poetry that will touch your heart and stir your soul. These verses speak to the theme of Universal Oneness, spiritual salvation and living your physical life to the fullest while in this realm. Open your mind, escape to silence, read and contemplate.

U. S. $8.95 / CAN. $13.00   ISBN: 0-9794585-1-X

"Psychic Princess: Admirable Avocation" by Jolinda Pizzirani is the first in a series about a young woman, "Danni," with psychic abilities who unwillingly gets involved in solving various crimes. In this first volume, Danni's good friend, Peggy, convinces her to use her capabilities to help find a rich couple's daughter who is missing without a clue. Danni reluctantly agrees to try her best, unsure if she will help--or hinder--the investigation. Who knows how her powers will affect her life and the lives of others?

U. S. $15.95 / CAN. $20.95   ISBN: 0-9794585-2-8

Order Any of These Great Books from:
www.summerlandpublishing.com, www.barnesandnoble.com, www.amazon.com
Or find them in your local bookstore or gift shop!
Email SummerlandPubs@aol.com for more information.